Birth and Early Years of Gandhiji's Life

Mahatma Gandhi is one of the most revered names in Indian history. He was the political and ideological leader of India, also honoured as Father of our nation, he became an international symbol of the free India. He played a very important role in the Indian freedom movement. He is lovingly called as Bapu. His teachings of 'Ahinsa' and 'Satya' (non-violence and truth) changed the complete outlook of the Indian freedom fighters.

Mohan Das Karamchand Gandhi, also known as Mahatma Gandhi, was born on 2nd October 1869 in a Hindu family of Porbandar, Gujarat. His parents were Karamchand Gandhi and Putlibai.

His father, Karamchand Gandhi was a Diwan (Chief Minister) of Porbandar and an honourable and upright man. Gandhiji's mother was a religious and pious woman. Gandhiji gained high moral and social values from his parents. Since childhood, Gandhiji believed strongly in non-violence, truth, purity and very simple lifestyle.

At the age of 13, Gandhiji got married to a girl of the same age named, Kasturba Gandhi. They had four sons. Gandhiji started his education in Porbandar. He further studied in Rajkot and did his matriculation. Then, he joined the University of Bombay in 1887. His family wanted him to become a barrister.

In 1888, he went to London for further studies and completed his law in 1891. He returned to India. For the next two years, he practised law in India.

Gandhiji in South Africa

At the age of 23, Gandhiji left his family once again and came to South Africa as a legal advisor of an Indian businessman. In South Africa, Gandhiji found that there was a strong demarcation between the Black and White communities. The Black community faced a lot of discrimination and were very badly treated. Gandhiji felt very bad about this.

Just after a week of his stay, Gandhiji experienced the humiliation because of discrimination. One day, he had to travel in a train. He had a first-class ticket with him. At the Pietermartizburg station when he entered the first-class compartment and was asked to shift to the third-class compartment. The ticket checker told him that the first-class was reserved for Whites.

On raising objection on this discrimination, Gandhiji was thrown out of the train.

During this journey, he late came to know
that discrimination is the common
practise there. The Black
community and the Indians
were called 'coolies'.

After this incident, Gandhiji decided to fight against this injustice. He wrote letters to the higher officials and began a protest against the discrimination in South Africa.

For the next three years, Gandhiji continuously fought for the justice. Soon, he became a well-known activist and a leader of the Indian community.

On 22nd May 1894, Gandhiji established an organisation—Natal Indian Congress (NIC) in South Africa. This organisation looked after the rights of Indians living there. While working for NIC, Gandhiji also faced a lot of opposition from the other communities. He was also attacked several times.

Gandhiji spent twenty years in South Africa. Thereafter, in the year 1915, he returned to India.

Gandhiji in India

Gandhiji's struggles and successes in South Africa were well known in India also. He became a 'National Hero' in the eyes of Indians. Gandhiji wanted to create the same wave of reformation in India. He travelled to all the parts of India to know the real conditions of Indians.

While his travels, Gandhiji used to wear a dhoti and wooden slippers. He renounced all the pleasures and adopted a very simple lifestyle.

He established the 'Sabarmati Ashram' in Ahmedabad, Gujarat. He lived in the ashram with his family and some of his supporters. Everyone loved and supported Gandhiji.

People started believing in his teachings of non-violence and truth. He got the title of 'Mahatma', which meant 'a great soul'.

The Indian Freedom Movement

India was under British rule at that time. A large number of freedom fighters were fighting for the freedom of India. Gandhiji also wanted the freedom of India but he followed a different path. He began a non-violent movement called 'Satyagraha' against the British.

Satyagraha means opposition, but not in an aggressive form. Gandhiji taught people to ask for justice in a silent way. The movement created a strong wave and became a great success.

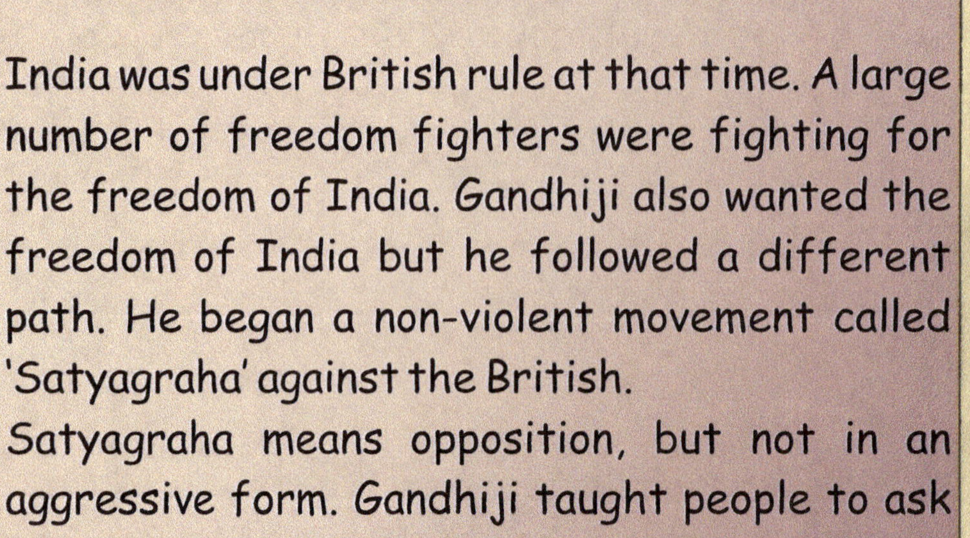

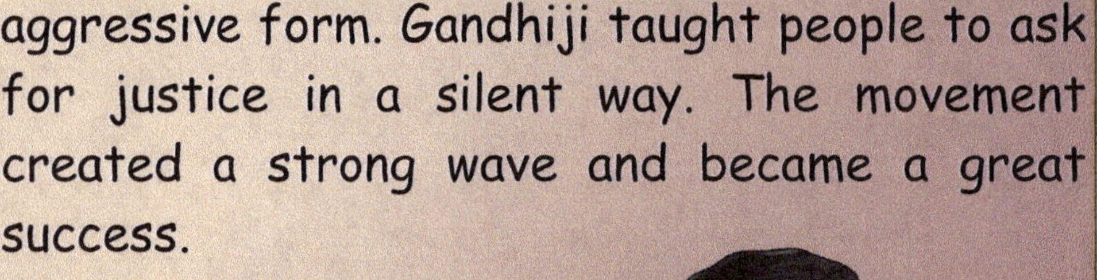

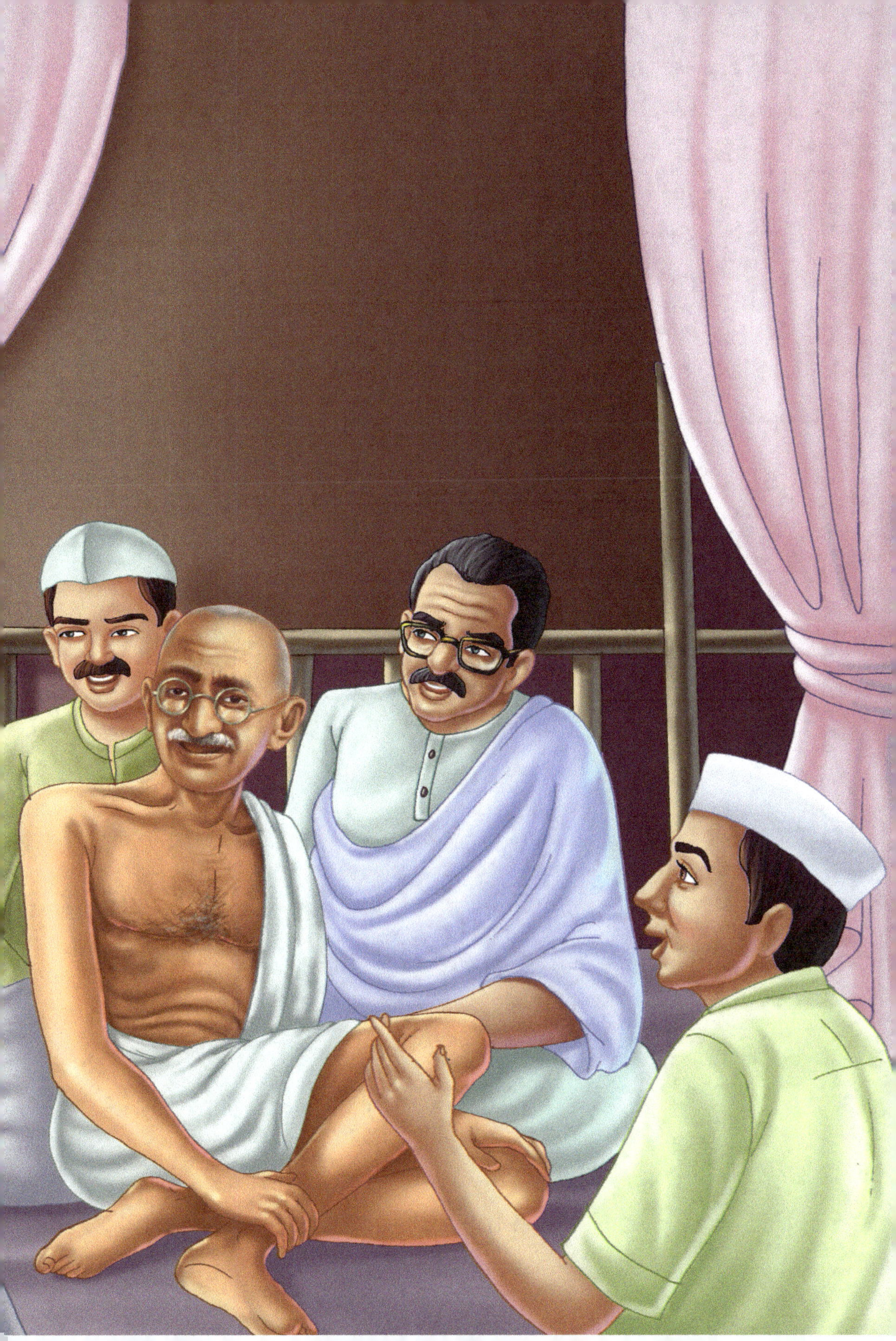

In 1919-20, Gandhiji started another movement called 'Non-cooperative movement'. During his struggle for freedom, Gandhiji was sent to jail many times by the British Govt, but he continued his mission. He asked indians to stop using foreign clothes and other things. He insisted to spin natural cloth on Charkha (spinning wheel). The image of the Charkha later became a symbol of the Indian independence.

On 12th March 1930, Gandhi ji began 'Dandi March' or the 'Salt March' against the salt tax. Gandhi ji with his supporters stand walking 200 miles from Sabarmati Ashram towards the sea.

On April 5, the group reached Dandi, a place along the Coast. Gandhiji demonstrated the method to make salt from the seawater. Soon, the movement spread in the entire nation. Gandhiji was imprisoned once again but, the protest continued nationwide. It was stopped only after the 'Delhi Pact' between the British Government and Gandhiji. The Pact granted the limited salt production and all the protestors were released.

In 1942, Gandhiji issued the last call for independence from British rule. He initiated another movement called 'August Kranti.' Soon after, he began 'Quit India' movement that asked the Britishers to leave India.

After the long struggle and sacrifices, India became independent on 15th August 1947. At the time of freedom, India faced the partition in two parts. After the freedom, Gandhiji tried to maintain peace and unity among the people of different communities.

There was a lot of disturbance in all the parts of country. The communal violence was spreading fast. To stop this violence, Gandhiji began a 'fast unto death' on 13th January 1948 which proved to be a success. On 18th January 1948, he ended his fast only when he got the assurance that the communal violence would be stopped.

Assassination of Gandhiji

Some Indians believed that Gandhiji was responsible for the partition of India. Gandhiji faced a lot of opposition. On the unfortunate day of 30th January 1948, Gandhiji was going to address a prayer meeting. He was walking along with his two assistants—Abha and Manu. Just when he was stepping towards the stage to address the public, a man named Nathuram Godse fired at Gandhiji.

Gandhiji fell on the ground, saying, "Hey Ram, Hey Ram!" These were the last words of Mahatma Gandhi.

The great soul, the light of the nation, was gone. The whole country was mourning bitterly on their dear Bapu's departure from the world. The other countries were also shocked at his death.

Soon after the assassination of Mahatma Gandhi, Pt. Jawahar Lal Nehru addressed the nation on radio:
"Friends & Comarades, The light has gone out of our lives and there is darkness everywhere. I do not know what to tell you and how to say it. Our beloved leader, Bapu as we called him, the Father of the Nation, is no more.
Perhaps I am wrong to say that. Nevertheless, we will never see him again as we have seen him for these many years. We will not run to him for advice and seek solace from him, and that is a terrible blow, not only to me, but also to millions and millions in this country.
And it is a little difficult to soften the blow by any other advice that I or anyone else can give you.."

India Remembers Mahatma Gandhi

Mahatma Gandhi's Samadhi is at Raj Ghat in Delhi. Thousands of people from all over the country come to Raj Ghat to pay homage to the great man.

2nd October, Gandhiji's birthday is celebrated as 'Gandhi Jayanti'. It is one of the three National festivals of India. People of India still remember their dear 'Bapu' with great love and reverence.

Every year, 30th January—the day of Gandhiji's assassination, is observed as the Martyr's Day to commemorate the struggle of all those who sacrificed their life for the country. Mahatma Gandhi's picture is also printed on the Indian currency notes.

Mahatma Gandhi was a great writer also. He wrote and edited many newspaper articles during his lifetime. He also wrote several books including his autobiography—My Experiments with Truth.

In the year 1930, Time magazine named Mahatma Gandhi as 'The Man of the Year'. There are many books written about him and his teachings. The life of Mahatma Gandhi has been widely portrayed in the Indian literature, theatre and movies.

Mahatma Gandhi dedicated his entire life for the welfare of Indians. He has been the greatest source of inspiration for all the Indians. His teachings of non-violence, peace and truth are still practised and followed by many, not only in India but also in other countries.

The only way to pay tribute to the great man—The Father of Our Nation—is to follow his teachings in our lives. We should learn from the great life of Mahatma Gandhi.

Birth and Early Years of Netaji's Life

Netaji Subhash Chandra Bose is considered as one of the most dynamic and revolutionary leader of Indian freedom struggle. He made and led the Azad Hind Fauj against the British rule and other western countries during the World War II. He was well known for his extraordinary courage and bold personality.

Netaji was born in a Bengali family on 23rd January 1897 in Cuttack, Orissa. His parents were Janakinath Bose and Prabhavati Devi. He was ninth of the fourteen children of his parents. His father was a successful advocate. Netaji was highly influenced by Swami Vivekanand and his teachings. During his college years, he attended many discourses of Swami Vivekanand.

Netaji was a brilliant student. He completed his school education in Cuttack. He was the topper of the Matriculation examination in the entire Calcutta province. In his student life, Netaji was known for his patriotic zeal. In his school, there used to be a lot of racial discrimination. The local students were target of the English students. The English boys always used to insult and torture the Indians.

One day, an English boy screamed at an Indian boy who touched his book. He said, "You black monkey! How dare you touch my book with your dirty hands."
The Indian boy was frightened. He could not say anything. He quietly listened to all the insulting remarks of the English boy. Netaji who was witnessing the incident, became very angry.

After the class, Netaji asked the Indian boy, "Why didn't you reply back to that English boy? He insulted you so badly!"
The Indian boy told Netaji that the English boy's father was a senior government officer. There could be negative consequences, if he would have fought with him.
Netaji was furious at the English boy. He confronted with him. The English boy made racial remarks on Netaji also. Netaji then caught him by his collar and thrashed him. The English boy fell on the ground.

This incident clearly proved that Netaji didn't fear from anyone. Since childhood, he was concerned about the dignity of his country and the countrymen.

Another such incident happened when Netaji was in college.

One day, a British professor made a racist remark on Indian students. Netaji became very angry and he beat the professor for the remark. After this incident, Netaji was expelled from the college.

Thereafter in 1918, he took a degree in philosophy from the University of Calcutta.

Netaji's parents wanted him to appear in the Civil Service Examination. To fulfil their wish, he went to England in the year 1919. He became successful and stood fourth in the merit of the Civil Service Examination.

Netaji had been a rebel since his childhood. He was against the British Rule in India. He didn't want to work under Britishers. When he came to know about Jalianwala Bagh Massacre in Punjab, he left his Civil Service apprenticeship and came back to India.

Netaji with Congress

On returning back to India, Netaji joined the Indian National Congress in Calcutta. He worked under the leadership of Deshbandhu Chittranjan Das. Netaji worked very hard to enlighten the youth and labour of Calcutta. Soon, he became a popular youth leader.

In November 1921, the Prince of Wales came to India to visit the country. The Indian National Congress decided to raise a protest against his visit. In Calcutta, Netaji organised a mass boycott to welcome the Prince.

In December 1921, Netaji and Chittranjan Das both were arrested and then imprisoned for six months. After their release, they continued working for their mission. The British Government was shocked to see Netaji's aggressive approach.

In 1924, Netaji stood for the municipal elections of Calcutta Corporation. He was elected as the Chief Executive and Chittranjan Das became the Mayor of Calcutta.

Soon, Netaji declared khadi in place of British mill-made cloth as the official dress. It was his first expression of the protest. The use of khadi was banned and Netaji was imprisoned in the Burma's Mandalay prison. This place was famous for its worst hygienic conditions. Netaji contracted Tuberculosis in the prison.

While Netaji was still in prison, his mentor and political guru Chittranjan Das passed away on 16th June 1925. Netaji was completely broken on hearing the news.

The following year, the State Council Election were held in Bengal. Netaji fought the election from the prison. He was declared elected from the Calcutta constituency. After a massive public protest and Netaji's hunger strike, he was finally released from the prison.

Netaji returned to Calcutta after his release in 1927. People, especially the youngsters, were very happy on his return.

In December 1927, Congress held its annual session in Madras. Netaji and Jawahar Lal Nehru were elected as General Secretaries of the Party.

Netaji was in favour of using violence and force to attain complete freedom. He opposed the Dominion status for India that was declared by the Congress. He said that, "We need complete independence and nothing else!"

He made a separate group named 'The Forward Bloc' within the party. This group organised nationwide rallies and protests. Because of this, he had disagreements with party officials. Finally, he left the Indian National Congress.

For his revolutionary thoughts, Netaji was imprisoned during the Civil Disobedience Movement in 1930. Netaji was exiled from India to Europe. But he used this opportunity and tried to establish political and cultural ties between India and Europe.

During his Vienna journey, he wrote a book, 'The Indian Struggle'. The book was published in November 1934. During the writing of this book Netaji met Miss Emily Shenkil. She assisted him in his writing. In 1937, Netaji got married to her. He could stay with his wife only for a month. Thereafter, he returned to India.

Netaji was arrested several times by the British Government. Later, he was kept in house arrest in Calcutta.

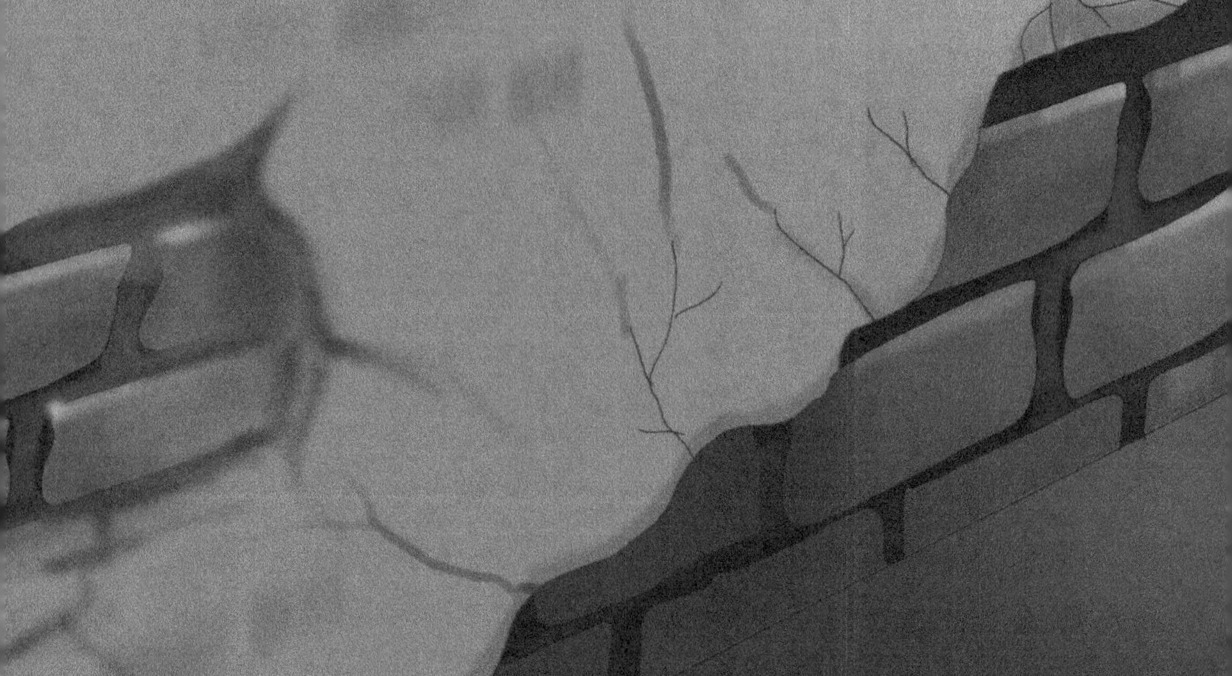

Netaji Forms the Indian National Army

At the time of the World War II, British were under the pressure of Adolf Hitler of Germany . Netaji took advantage of the situation. Disguised as a Pathan (Pashtun), he fled from Calcutta to Peshawar in 1941. From there, he went to Kabul and then to Moscow.

Netaji's next destination was Germany. He reached there and met Hitler. He told Hitler about his cause. Hitler was quite impressed by Netaji and promised to help.

In 1941, Netaji went to Japan. He got the support of Germany and Japan for his fight against the British rule in India. In 1943, he moved to Singapore and formed the Indian National Army (INA). The army was also called the Azad Hind Fauj. Netaji became the Commander-in-Chief of the Azad Hind Fauj.

The army comprised mainly of the Indian prisoners of war (POW).

There were around 40,000 soldiers. The army was made up of four brigades—The Nehru Brigade, The Gandhi Brigade, The Subhash Brigade and The Azad Brigade. There was also a women's unit named Rani Jhansi Regiment. It consisted of 100 women soldiers.

Netaji prepared the army for the battle. In 1944, INA crossed the Burma border and reached India. It waged a battle against the British Rule from the Northwest part of India. The army enthusiastically moved forward with the battle cry, 'Chalo Dilli!'

During the World War II, Germany and Japan were defeated. Because of this, the Azad Hind Fauj battle was not a success, but Netaji conveyed the message to the British. The British Government realised that Indians can go to any extent for the freedom of their country.

In one of his inspiring speeches, he said, "Tum mujhe khoon do, main tumhein azadi doonga!" (Give me your blood, and I'll give you freedom!). This quote of Netaji became very popular and inspired the Indians to a great extent.

Netaji also visited England. He met many significant political leaders. He also discussed about the future of the Indian freedom movement with them.

Netaji's Disappearance

On 18th August 1945, Netaji was travelling in a private plane to Tokyo, Japan. Over Taipei, Taiwan, the plane caught fire and crashed. Netaji was declared dead in the plane crash. But later, it was found that Netaji's body was not there among the victims.

A lot of questions and doubts were raised about Netaji's death. A special committee was also formed to investigate the truth. But no evidence of his death was found. Some people believed that Netaji was alive even after the incident. However, no strong evidence was there. Hence, Netaji's death has been a mystery for India.

Netaji Subhash Chandra Bose left a strong impression on the minds of Indians. Unfortunately, he could not witness the moment of Indian independence, for which he struggled very hard.

Netaji Subhash Chandra Bose played a very significant role in the freedom movement of India. His inspirational words, quotes and speeches are still remembered and ignite patriotic emotions in the Indians.

We can learn a lot from Netaji's life. His qualities like- patriotic zeal, courage and boldness are unmatchable.